DATE DUE

FEB 0 7 2008	

Quanah Parker

History Maker Bios

Shannon Zemlicka

LERNER PUBLICATIONS COMPANY • MINNEAPOLIS

Map on p. 9 by Laura Westlund
Illustrations by Tim Parlin

Lerner Publications Company
A division of Lerner Publishing Group
241 First Avenue North
Minneapolis, MN 55401 U.S.A.

Website address: www.lernerbooks.com

Library of Congress Cataloging-in-Publication Data

Zemlicka, Shannon.
    Quanah Parker / by Shannon Zemlicka.
       p.   cm. — (History maker bios)
    Summary: A biography of Quanah Parker, a spiritual and political leader of the Comanche people in the late nineteenth and early twentieth centuries. Includes bibliographical references and index.
       ISBN: 0–8225–0724–2 (lib. bdg. : alk. paper)
    1. Parker, Quanah, 1845?–1911—Juvenile literature. 2. Comanche Indians—Biography—Juvenile literature. [1. Parker, Quanah, 1845?–1911. 2. Comanche Indians—Biography. 3. Indians of North America—Biography. 4. Kings, queens, rulers, etc.] I. Title. II. Series.
E99.C85P389 2004
976.4004'9745—dc21   2003005624

Manufactured in the United States of America
1 2 3 4 5 6 – JR – 09 08 07 06 05 04

TABLE OF CONTENTS

INTRODUCTION

Quanah Parker was a warrior, a rancher, a judge, a religious leader, and a businessman. He was an unusual person in an unusual time.

Quanah was born in northern Texas around 1849. He grew up in a band of Comanche on America's southern plains. The Comanche called themselves the People. They were one of America's many Native American nations. During Quanah's lifetime, soldiers forced the People to move to a small piece of land called a reservation.

Quanah spent many years trying to help the People live as well as they could on the reservation. He didn't always succeed. But he lived an amazing life.

This is his story.

1 SON OF THE PEOPLE

As a boy, Quanah (KWAH-nah) often went to sleep hungry. So did his father, a strong war chief named Peta Nocona, and his blue-eyed mother, Naudah. Peta Nocona hunted well. But hunting was harder for the People than it used to be.

Every year, more white people came to settle the land where the People lived. They built houses, forts, and towns on the People's hunting grounds. Animals had less living space—and more hunters chasing them. Sometimes everyone went hungry.

Quanah learned quickly that the buffalo was the most important animal to the People. Almost every part of a buffalo could be eaten. Buffalo hides could be used to make clothes or cover for tipis. These cone-shaped shelters provided warm, dry places to sleep.

The People often moved their camps during hunting season. Tipis were made to be easily taken down and set up again.

Depending on the buffalo meant living on the move. Buffalo roamed in herds, traveling in search of grass to eat. Quanah and the band moved with them. Sometimes life was hard. But Quanah felt safe and loved with his parents to care for him.

Every boy learned to hunt as soon as he was able. At an early age, Quanah could shoot arrows with a small bow. He could ride a pony with speed and skill by the time he was about five years old.

QUICKSAND RESCUE

One day when Quanah was about nine, the band was crossing a river. Quanah's pony began to sink in quicksand. Quanah loved the pony and refused to leave it behind. He began to sink too. Just in time, a man rushed up and threw a rope around the pony's neck. The man pulled both Quanah and the pony to safety.

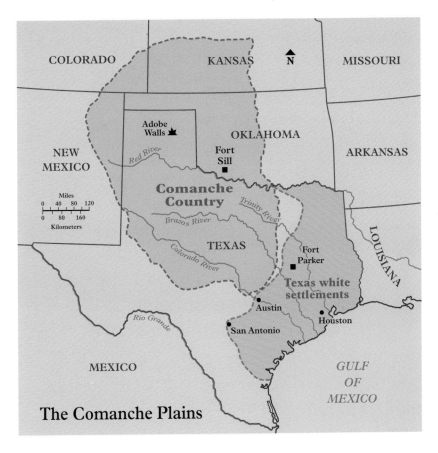

The Comanche Plains

Quanah learned to fight too. The People needed protection from their enemies, and they needed brave men who could round up horses and drive away invaders. Quanah became skilled with a shield and a long, sharp pole called a lance.

He grew up surrounded by the traditions of the People. His mother told him stories of the Great Spirit and the creation of the world.

Quanah learned to hunt with a bow and arrow.

One tradition Quanah learned was the peyote religion. Peyote is a small type of cactus. Native Americans of many nations used it in sacred ceremonies.

A person who ate dried peyote saw visions—pictures in the mind. The People believed these visions brought them closer to the Great Spirit and healed the sick.

Quanah was about twelve years old when something terrible happened. It was 1860. Quanah had gone hunting with his younger brother, Peenah, and his father. Two riders brought news. White soldiers had raided the women and children's camp.

The soldiers had killed many people. Worst of all for Quanah, they had taken Naudah, his mother. His baby sister, Topsannah, was gone as well.

Peta Nocona couldn't rescue Naudah and Topsannah. Too many soldiers had taken them. The kind, blue-eyed mother who had fed Quanah, made his clothes, and told him stories was gone for good.

Peta Nocona had two wives besides Naudah. The soldiers had killed one. The other helped care for Quanah and Peenah.

Quanah missed his mother very much after she was taken from the People.

About three years later, Peta Nocona told Quanah something he had never known about his mother. Naudah was white. Peta Nocona had captured her in a raid on a white settlement in Texas. She was a girl then, a nine-year-old called Cynthia Ann Parker. She grew up as a woman of the People, and Peta Nocona married her.

Finally, Quanah understood why his mother had blue eyes instead of brown ones, like the rest of the People had. The white soldiers who had stolen his mother were her own people. And if his mother was white, he must be half white.

Naudah was captured as a young girl when Fort Parker was raided by Comanche warriors.

Quanah's father died soon after he told Quanah the truth about Naudah. Then Peenah died as well. For a while, Peta Nocona's third wife still helped provide for Quanah. When she died too, he was truly alone.

Life became harder. Many of the People looked down on Quanah because he was half white. He often had to beg for food and clothing. He decided to prove his worth in the one way everyone respected—in battle.

2 WAR CHIEF

Quanah joined other young men on raids in Texas and Mexico. The warriors stole horses and goods. Often they captured or killed enemies. Sometimes they fought American soldiers too.

In 1867, Quanah went to Kansas for a gathering of Native Americans from many nations. Officials from the United States government were there too. The officials said the Native Americans must stop raiding and fighting. They must become farmers on land the government set aside for them. This land was called a reservation. It was much smaller than the land where the People had followed the buffalo for years.

A Comanche war party rides out from their camp on horseback.

The United States government would give the Native Americans clothes, houses, and schools on the reservation. For a while, the government would give money and food too. But the Native Americans would have to give up their homeland forever so that white people could live there.

Some of the People's bands took the offer. They were tired of fighting soldiers. Maybe they would find a better life on the reservation. They signed a treaty, a written agreement with the government.

A DANGEROUS PIECE OF WOOD

One night, Quanah and his men were running away from a group of soldiers. The warriors stopped in the woods to sleep. One spotted a soldier sleeping beneath a tree. Everyone was too nervous to go any closer. But Quanah crept up, ready to strike. The "soldier" turned out to be a fallen log!

A long feather headdress was a sign of honor for a Comanche warrior.

Quanah wanted nothing to do with the treaty. He wanted to remain a warrior and hunt buffalo. The Quahada band felt the same way. Quanah left Kansas with them.

In 1869, Quanah went on a raid in southwest Texas. The raiders stole several horses. A group of white men with powerful shotguns came after them. The warriors decided to run.

Quanah wasn't afraid of anyone's guns, though. He slowed his horse and hid in some bushes by the trail. When two of the white men passed by, he rushed out and killed them with his spear.

Quanah's bravery impressed the other warriors. They made him a war chief. He could lead men into battles and on raids, as his father had done. Quanah had earned the respect he longed for.

As a war chief, Quanah stole horses, fought settlers and soldiers, and took prisoners. Most chiefs killed the white men they captured. Women and children were beaten. But Quanah didn't harm his prisoners. Maybe he remembered his mother, who had been a prisoner of both the People and white soldiers.

U.S. soldiers were sent by the government to drive Native Americans off traditional lands.

Eagles are strong and fierce birds. Their feathers are important symbols to the People.

By 1871, most of the People's bands had agreed to go to the reservation where the American government wanted them to live. The government sent soldiers to force the Quahadas to go too.

Quanah was determined to guard his band's freedom. One day in October, Quahada scouts spotted soldiers camped on the White River in Texas. The band needed time to escape to safe ground.

The next day, Quanah led an attack on the soldiers as the band fled. The very sight of him filled his enemies with fear. He wore black war paint and a necklace of bear claws. A huge war bonnet of eagle feathers covered his head and swept down almost to the ground. Bells and bits of red cloth decorated his horse.

The Quahadas fought hard. They ran to catch up with the band, but the soldiers followed them. Then Quanah had an idea. He made false tracks. The soldiers went the wrong way, and the Quahadas escaped. For the time being, their war chief's bravery and cleverness had kept them safe.

3 ON THE RUN

Even though the soldiers posed great danger to the Quahadas, in some ways, life went on as it always had. Quanah had gathered a large herd of horses, making him a wealthy man. He was ready to start a family.

Quanah often wore a traditional Comanche breastplate like this one.

In 1872, he married twice. His first wife was an Apache who missed her home too much to stay with him. His second wife, Weckeah, was a young woman of the People. She gave birth to Quanah's first child, a daughter.

Times were getting harder for the Quahada band. More white settlers had built homes on the land the People roamed. White hunters killed thousands of buffalo every day. The animals the People depended on for food and clothing became harder to find.

Quanah and other warriors kept raiding white settlements. They hoped to scare away the settlers who were stealing the People's land. But the more the warriors raided, the angrier the settlers and soldiers became. Many people from both sides died.

In 1874, Quanah helped a war party attack buffalo hunters at Adobe Walls, a trading post in Texas. After this fight, more soldiers came after the Quahadas.

At the time of the Battle of Adobe Walls, the trading post was a small collection of sod buildings.

For a year, the band lived on the run. They camped in a hiding place until the band's scouts spotted the soldiers. Then the women packed the tipis, and the band hurried on. Living this way made it harder than ever to find food. The Quahadas became miserable.

In 1875, American soldiers offered the Quahadas a chance to give up. If they came to the reservation, they would not be hurt. If they refused to come, the soldiers would hunt them until they were all dead.

KILLING THE BUFFALO

Why did white hunters kill so many buffalo? The animals' hides and tongues could be sold for a great deal of money. The U.S. Army probably could have stopped the hunting. But they wanted the buffalo gone so that Native Americans, such as the People, would have nothing to hunt and would have to move to reservations.

After the Battle of Adobe Walls, some Comanche fled to the canyons of northern Texas and western Oklahoma.

Quanah climbed to high ground to think about what to do. The choice wasn't his alone. But the band's other leaders would listen to his thoughts. If the band kept running and fighting, they would probably starve or be killed by soldiers. Quanah believed that dying in battle was a good end for a warrior. He would rather die fighting than give up. But the women and children would die too.

Quanah remembered his mother. As a child, his father had taken her from the world of white settlers. She had learned to live as one of the People. Maybe Quanah could learn to live a new way as well.

The Comanche believed that certain animals, such as wolves, could guide people in making important decisions.

In the distance, he saw a wolf. It howled toward him, then turned northeast. Quanah knew that the reservation lay in that direction. An eagle flew past. It, too, changed course to the northeast.

Quanah believed he had been shown the path he must follow. Soon after that day, he spoke in favor of going to the reservation. The other Quahada leaders agreed. The band traveled to Fort Sill, Oklahoma. There they surrendered to the U.S. Army. Their days of wandering the open plains had ended for good.

4 A NEW LIFE

As soon as Quanah got to the
reservation, he asked for information
about his mother, Naudah. He learned that
she had died a few years before.
Topsannah, Quanah's little sister, had also
died. He would have to find his own way in
his new home.

Almost every part of the Quahadas' life changed. The reservation had no buffalo or other game animals. The men couldn't hunt for food. The government sent some food, but often there wasn't enough to keep all the families well fed.

Another problem was cattle. Many white people raised cattle on huge ranches. Some ranchers brought their herds across the reservation on their way to market. The reservation was supposed to be for Native Americans. But it was hard to stop the huge herds from stomping through the reservation.

NAUDAH AND TOPSANNAH

The soldiers who captured Naudah realized that she was Cynthia Ann Parker. She and Topsannah were sent to live with relatives in Texas. Naudah tried several times to escape and return to her Comanche family. She never succeeded. Topsannah was a happy child, but she died of sickness in 1864. Naudah died a few years later.

Quanah began to dress like the white ranchers who moved cattle through the reservation.

Quanah saw a way to solve both problems. Since this land belonged to the People, they could charge the cattle ranchers to cross it. Then the People would have money for food. And they would have important new friends in the cattle ranchers.

It took a long time to work out a plan that the ranchers, government leaders, and Native Americans agreed on. Quanah even traveled to Washington, D.C., in 1884 to talk with American leaders. In the end, all of the People received some money from the ranchers each year. In exchange, the ranchers could take their cattle across the reservation.

This photograph marks a meeting between Quanah and Andrew Jackson Houston, a U.S. government official.

Quanah discovered that talking with white men about money and land came easily to him. On the plains, he had been good at making war and leading raids. Here on the reservation, he was good at making friends—and making deals. He believed that by doing both, he could help the People survive.

Quanah became a cattle rancher himself by using his money to buy a herd. He began to use his mother's last name, Parker. Taking this name honored Naudah and his history as a person of two races. It also reminded the white men who ran the reservation that he was as much white as Native American.

Those white men began to see Quanah as the main leader of the people they called Comanche. They made Quanah a judge on the reservation's court in 1886.

Quanah became an important leader on the reservation. Here he poses with schoolchildren and their teachers.

Quanah hoped to lead his people toward change. He believed that to survive on the reservation, the People had to live as white people did. That meant speaking English, sending children to school, and earning money by farming or ranching.

Still, he didn't want everything to change. One tradition he kept was the peyote religion. Quanah believed the People needed the comfort of this religion more than ever. But some government officials tried to keep the People from using peyote. They wanted them to become Christians, as many white people were.

Peyote is a type of cactus that grows in Texas and Mexico.

One of Quanah's daughters looks doubtful about having her picture taken.

Quanah didn't show his support of the peyote religion openly. That would have created trouble for him. But he secretly became a leader of peyote ceremonies. He worked to make sure that peyote was shipped to the reservation. He even spread the religion to other reservations when he traveled.

Quanah also followed the tradition that allowed a man to marry more than one woman. By 1890, he had five wives. He married twice more during the 1890s. Over time, he became the father of twenty-two children. The Parker family lived in a huge white house with stars painted on the roof.

Quanah's family all lived in the roomy Star House in Cache, Oklahoma, near Fort Sill.

Quanah had built a new life. He was wealthy and had the respect of both the People and the American government. But a new trouble came in 1892. Like many of the People's troubles, this one involved land.

The government had a new plan for the reservation. This land had been promised to Native Americans forever. But white settlers wanted more land for farms. The government decided the Native Americans didn't need all their land. Each would be given a small farm. The government would buy the rest of the land from the Native Americans and sell it to white settlers.

Quanah didn't want to sell the land. Most of the other chiefs didn't either. But they were told that the government would buy the land by force if the chiefs refused. Then the price would be whatever the government wanted to pay. To be sure of a good price, the chiefs must sign an agreement.

Quanah saw no way out. He did what he had done many times over the years. He tried to get the best deal for the People. He asked for more money and more time before the land would be sold. Then, when he could do nothing more, he signed the agreement. The other chiefs did the same.

The People would soon lose their land to the United States—again.

5 LEADING THE PEOPLE

Quanah tried for years to put off the sale of the reservation land to white settlers. He traveled with other chiefs to Washington, D.C., to argue the People's case. But he was told that the land would still be sold.

Another blow came in 1898. It was against the law in the United States to have more than one wife. As a judge, Quanah was supposed to live by the law. So a government official decided that he could no longer be a judge unless he lived with only one wife.

Quanah couldn't imagine giving up any part of his family. How could he send away any of the wives he loved? How could he send away his own children? When he refused, he was fired from his job as a judge.

Quanah and his wife Weckeah pose for a portrait.

Still, in many ways Quanah's life was good. His family kept growing and thriving. He had enough cattle and money to share with his friends. And in 1899, the government gave him the title of principal chief of the Comanche. This title didn't mean that Quanah could give orders or make all decisions for the People. It simply meant that the government understood him to be the People's most important leader.

Quanah didn't have enough power to keep out the white settlers who wanted reservation land, though. They came at last in 1901.

Fort Sill, Oklahoma, was part of the white settlement of the southern plains.

Quanah (STANDING, FAR RIGHT) poses with other Native American leaders on a trip to Washington, D.C.

Quanah lost the huge pasture where his cattle had grazed. And the People no longer received payments from white ranchers for cattle to graze on the reservation.

By this time, Quanah was about fifty-two years old. His leadership had made him known throughout the United States as a wise chief who had traded a life of war for one of peace. Many towns invited him to appear in parades and give speeches, especially in Texas.

Quanah had no interest in being stared at like an animal in a zoo. But he loved to travel, so he went to many parades. Most of all, he loved to put on his old feather headdress and show what a warrior of the People had looked like.

One of the parades he rode in took place in Washington, D.C. It celebrated the election of a new American president, Theodore Roosevelt. Quanah made friends with Roosevelt. Later that year, the two men hunted together on the reservation. Quanah was honored to host the president for dinner at his house.

QUANAH'S BRAIDS

When the government banned braids for Native American men, Quanah refused to cut his. He pointed out that one official had a Chinese servant who wore his hair in a braid. This was a Chinese tradition. Why couldn't Quanah follow his people's tradition too? The official had no answer to this. Quanah kept his braids.

Quanah built these memorials (CENTER AND RIGHT) to his mother Naudah and sister Topsannah.

As he grew older, he kept working to protect the peyote religion. He helped lawmakers understand why the plant should not be banned.

He had one final wish, to find his mother's grave and have her remains buried in Oklahoma. He placed ads in newspapers, asking for help. To his delight, a white cousin wrote to him. Quanah was able to find both Naudah's and Topsannah's graves. In 1910, his mother and sister were reburied among the graves of the People.

Quassiah (LEFT) was a close friend of Quanah. He spoke at a 1926 ceremony dedicating a monument to Quanah in Oklahoma.

Just a few months later, in 1911, Quanah died. He was about sixty-two years old. Buried beside Naudah, he was at last reunited with the mother he had lost.

Quanah was the last principal chief of the People. The American government never gave another chief this title. The modern Comanche nation has no chief. Their leader is a chairman who is elected through voting.

The peyote religion that Quanah helped protect came to be called the Native American Church. It has more than 250,000 members. Their use of peyote is protected by law.

Quanah Parker lived two lives in two worlds. He led his people through many difficult changes. He became a success, yet he never gave up the traditions he valued most.

TIMELINE

QUANAH PARKER WAS PROBABLY BORN AROUND 1849.

In the year . . .

1854   Quanah could ride a pony and shoot arrows with a small bow.

1860   his mother and little sister were kidnapped by Texas soldiers.   Age 11

1863   he learned that his mother was white.

1867   he went to a gathering where American officials said that the People must move to a reservation.

1869   he became a war chief of the Quahada band.   Age 20

1871   he began to fight U.S. soldiers to keep the Quahadas free.

1872   he married his first two wives.

1874   he attacked buffalo hunters at Adobe Walls, Texas.

1875   the Quahadas agreed to go to a reservation in Oklahoma.   Age 26

1884   he traveled to Washington, D.C., to help work out a deal with cattle ranchers.

1886   he became a judge on the reservation court.

1898   he lost his job as a judge because he would not give up his wives.

1899   the U.S. government gave him the title of principal chief of the Comanche Indians.   Age 50

1901   he lost his land when the government took parts of the reservation for white settlers.

1910   he moved the graves of his mother and sister to join those of the People.

1911   he died on the reservation.   Age 62

TWO FAMILIES TOGETHER

When Quanah died, he left behind two families. His Comanche children lived on the reservation in Oklahoma. Many of them grew up to have children of their own. Back in Texas, Naudah's family—the white Parkers—grew as well. For many years, the two families did not talk or visit one another.

That changed in the 1950s. Both families knew that they had an important bond, their link to Quanah. To honor that bond, they began to hold family reunions. At these gatherings, the members of each family could get to know one another better. Now the families hold two reunions each year, one in Oklahoma and one in Texas. Each year at the Star House, Quanah's white and Comanche relatives exchange a bowl as a symbol of their shared history.

FURTHER READING

NONFICTION

Bial, Raymond. *The Comanche.* **New York: Benchmark Books, 2000.** An introduction to the history, culture, and modern life of the Comanche.

Lund, Bill. *The Comanche Indians.* **Mankato, MN: Bridgestone Books, 1997.** A brief look at Comanche history and culture.

Schwartz, Michael. *LaDonna Harris.* **Austin, TX: Raintree/Steck Vaughn, 1997.** A biography of a modern Comanche leader.

Streissguth, Thomas. *The Comanche.* **San Diego: Lucent Books, 2000.** The story of Comanche life on the plains and on the reservation.

FICTION

Dearen, Patrick. *Comanche Peace Pipe.* **Plano, TX: Republic of Texas Press, 2001.** A Comanche boy and a white boy become friends in Texas in 1867.

WEBSITES

Comanche Nation
<http://www.comanchenation.com/> Read about the history and modern government of the Comanche.

Comanche Stories
<http://www.comanchelodge.com/story.htm> Follow the links on this site to read Comanche tales of the creation of the world, the arrival of buffalo, and Quanah's romance with Weckeah.

Handbook of Texas Online: Comanche Indians
<http://www.tsha.utexas.edu/handbook/online/articles/vie
w/CC/bmc72.html> This article tells the role the Comanche
played in Texas history.

Quanah Parker Family Site of Cache, Oklahoma
<http://home.att.net/~ronparker/wsb/html/view.cgi-
home.html-.html> Some of Quanah's descendants hold
reunions at his home each year. Follow the "photos" link to
see photographs of his grandchildren and great-
grandchildren.

Select Bibliography

Exley, Jo Ella Powell. *Frontier Blood: The Saga of the
Parker Family*. College Station, TX: Texas A&M
University Press, 2001.

Fehrenbach, T. R. *Comanches: The Destruction of a People*.
New York: Da Capo Press, 1994.

Foster, Morris W. *Being Comanche: A Social History of an
American Indian Community*. Tucson, AZ: University of
Arizona Press, 1991.

Hagan, William T. *Quanah Parker, Comanche Chief*.
Norman, OK: University of Oklahoma Press, 1993.

Neeley, Bill. *The Last Comanche Chief: The Life and Times
of Quanah Parker*. New York: John Wiley and Sons,
1995.

Tilghman, Zoe. *Quanah, the Eagle of the Comanches*.
Oklahoma City, OK: Harlow Publishing, 1938.

INDEX

Acknowledgments

For photographs and artwork: © Western History Collections, University of Oklahoma Libraries, pp. 4, 7, 11, 29, 31, 33, 37, 45; © Historical Picture Archive/ CORBIS, p. 10; Photo courtesy Texas Parks & Wildlife © 2003, p. 12; Smithsonian American Art Museum, Washington, DC/ Art Resource, NY, p. 15; © Bettman/ CORBIS, p. 17, 39; © Geoffrey Clements/CORBIS, p. 18; PhotoDisc Royalty Free by Getty Images, pp. 19, 26; © Smithsonian Institution, p. 22; © Panhandle Plains Historical Museum, pp. 23, 30; © David Muench/CORBIS, p. 25; Smithsonian Institution National Anthropological Archives, Bureau of American Ethnology Collection, p. 32; Courtesy of Quanah Parker Society, ronparker@att.net, pp. 34, 41; Library of Congress (LC 6SZ62-093050), p. 38; Denver Public Library, Western History Department, p. 42. Front cover, © Western History Collections, University of Oklahoma Libraries. Back cover, © Historical Picture Archive/CORBIS.